Ladies First

How to Effectively Love Your Lady

Shawn McBride

Ladies First

Copyright © 2021 by Shawn McBride

All rights reserved. No part of this book may be reproduced or transmitted in any form or by any means without written permission from the author.

ISBN 9798729153893

TABLE OF CONTENTS

Introduction 11

Chapter 1 - Sacrificial Love 15

Chapter 2 - Selfless Love 21

Chapter 3 - Serving Love 27

Chapter 4 - Scorching Love 35

Chapter 5 - Sensitive Love 41

Chapter 6 - Secure Love 47

Chapter 7 - Loving Her Seed 51

Chapter 8 - Signs of Love 58

Conclusion 62

References 63

Dedication

I dedicate this book to my sons Jeremiah and Zachariah. I desire that whatever woman they choose to marry; they would passionately pursue them until death does them part.

Disclaimer

These are fictional stories to illustrate what happens in real-life relationships. All names have been changed not to reflect any couple I have personally provided counseling services for over the past two decades.

Introduction

Where did the concept 'Ladies First' originate?

On March 31, 2007, R&B sensation Musiq Soulchild released a song entitled "Teach Me." The song became an instant hit! The song peaked at number two on the Hot R&B/Hip-Hop Songs chart on July 14, 2007, a position it held for a total of five non-consecutive weeks. It tied the record set by Robin Thicke's "Lost Without U" for the longest run at number one on the U.S. Urban A.C. chart at 13 weeks.[1]

The lyrics to the song starts as follows:

> *[Verse 1]*
> *I was told the true definition of a man was to never cry*
> *Work till you tired (yeah), got to provide (yeah)*
> *Always be the rock for my fam, protect them by all means*
> *And give you the things that you need, baby*
> *Our relationship is (Suffering). Trying to give you (what I never had)*
> *You say I don't know how to love you, baby. Well, I say, show me the way*
> *I keep my feelings deep inside; I shadow them with my pride*
> *I'm trying desperately. Baby just work with me*
>
> *[Chorus]*

Teach me how to love.
Show me the way to surrender my heart.
Girl, I'm so lost, teach me how to love.
How I can get my emotions involved.
Teach me, show me how to love
Show me the way to surrender my heart
Girl, I'm so lost, teach me how to love.
How I can get my emotions involved.
Teach me how to love
Men need to be taught how to love a woman.
What you don't' know, you don't know

When explaining how the song came to be, Musiq said that we believe women should be emotional, but men showing the same side of themselves will emasculate him. *"Men don't get taught to sit alone with their thoughts. We teach boys and men that they need to be active, that they need to be doing; we don't really teach them to reflect on what they're feeling or what they're thinking about."*[2]

Musiq said he was taught to be the masculine head of the household and not show emotion. In his current relationship, though, he realized this would cost him the woman he loves, and this song is his expression of love to her, asking for her help to teach him what he needs to know to love her.

What Musiq used music and lyrics to do for him, I hope this book does for all the men out there. This book is intended to teach men how to effectively love a woman, meet the particular needs they have of us and pursue a lifetime of amazing relationship moments.

Women desperately desire to be loved, and men desire to be respected. There is a difference. Those differences draw us together and yet can drive us from relationships if there is no meeting of needs on both sides. This book is intended, by no means, to be an exhaustive book of tips to show your woman that you love and respect them; it's just the cliff notes version of how to make those critical steps that can mean the difference in a life-changing relationship and ending up alone – again!

Real males never embrace a victim mentality; instead, they take responsibility for their actions, mistakes, failures, and sins. If you want to lead the team, you must prove you can handle the ball. Be Responsible! If an archer shoots an arrow and misses the target, he looks within himself to find fault, not at the target. To improve your aim, you must improve yourself. Be responsible and stop making excuses. This book is a good foundation for taking on that responsibility and making an effort toward the relationship you desire.

Chapter 1

Sacrificial Love

Love Your Wife/Gave Up His Life-Ephesians 5

The Bruno Mars Song, *Grenade*[3], has a chorus that resonates with what you should be willing to give up for your lady.

> *[Chorus]*
> *I'd catch a grenade for ya (Yeah, yeah, yeah)*
> *Throw my hand on a blade for ya (Yeah, yeah, yeah)*
> *I'd jump in front of a train for ya (Yeah, yeah, yeah)*
> *You know I'd do anything for ya (Yeah, yeah, yeah)*
> *Oh-oh, oh, I would go through all this pain*
> *Take a bullet straight through my brain*
> *Yes, I would die for ya, baby*
> *But you won't do the same.*

> *Ephesians 5:25 (NLT) "For husbands, this means love your wives, just as Christ loved the church. He gave up His life for her."*

Short Story for Consideration

Jim had a truly rough day in court and came home on edge, needing to de-stress after the day. Mary comes home to find that Jim immediately starts asking only about dinner, bills paid, and the like after a long day at work. When he doesn't like the answers he received, he huffs off to the television to prop his feet up, as he has had a tough day and thinks it would be best, he separates from Mary to avoid a fight. Mary, of course, is hurt, bothered by the reaction, and sluggishly tries to finish up dinner and hurry into her home office to take care of what she needs to finish. The conversation is stilted, and then at bedtime, they turn from each other to sleep, waking in similar moods instead of being refreshed.

Means Sacrificial Love

If I were to describe how a man's love for a woman looks, I would draw a crucifix in the shape of a cross. To a Christian, a cross is a symbol of sacrifice and a reminder of the sacrifice Jesus Christ made on the cross to save sinners.

Sacrifice asks these questions: How can I serve my lady? How can I meet the needs that my lady has? How can I provide all that she needs? How can I make this relationship the best?

The Scripture places that burden firmly on the man's shoulders when It instructs him to love his wife like Christ loved the church. As we all know, Christ literally died on the cross to prove His love for all the people He would never meet. What are you willing to do to prove your sacrificial love for the lady you profess to love?

Verse 25 of Ephesians does not say rule over your wife; it doesn't say order her around by telling her what to do, it doesn't say make demands, it doesn't say conquer her or try to dominate her. It says love your wives in no uncertain terms, in the sacrificial way that Christ, by example, taught us to love.

The word for love used in Ephesians 5:25 is "agape," and it's the most intense, most divine, most magnanimous, most sacrificial, most humble kind of love; it's the love of the will. There are other words for love in the Greek language, but none with this importance in our lives.

Greek words for love[4]

1. Eros, or sexual passion
2. Philia, or deep friendship
3. Ludus, or playful love
4. Agape, or love for everyone
5. Pragma, or longstanding love
6. Philautia, or love of the self

Agape is the most overarching, maybe hardest of all loves to exercise, as it is the love of the will. This is a word for love that is not defined by the solicitation of the one loved. This is loving because it is right to love, loving because you will love. It doesn't mean the person is not attractive, but it is defined as a word that expresses one's intentionality.[5] It might be best described as a sentimental love demonstrated in action.[6] This means Christ allowed Himself to be placed on that cross and suffer immeasurable cruelty to prove His love. What are your actions saying to your lady about how you love her?

Sacrifice Not Selfishness

Back to the Scripture in Ephesians, a husband is instructed to give up his life for his wife. This spirit-filled husband loves his wife not for what she can do for him but for what he can do for her. Find a woman that you can love; find a woman that you are determined to love. Find a woman to whom you can give your life, and all your abilities, and all your powers, and all your energies, in the way Christ did for the church; a love that knows no tyranny, it only knows sacrifice. Christ loved the church and gave Himself up for her; find a woman and give yourself up for her.

Work harder to provide for her physical needs. Invest in her spiritually. Care for her, shelter her, protect her, provide for her, preserve her. Give your life for her. Find one who loves Christ, who should be under the care of a man, who should be under the protection of a husband, and become that to her that Christ is to His church. This is the sacrifice that defines what a husband does. By the way, love is always a verb, no exception. It is always in action, it is always in motion, and a Spirit-filled love is a love that is always sacrificing on behalf of another person.

Interesting to note here is that most men will expect women, per biblical insights, to submit to them. Think about this sacrificial love here mentioned, though. You are in charge of loving your wife, providing for your wife, meeting your wife's needs to the degree that Christ did for the church. In other words, submitting fully to the needs of the one to whom you are sacrificing, and in turn, fulfilling the greatest sacrifice humans can make in loving another more than ourselves. Those are some big strong words, and it takes a strong, secure, and centered man to meet them.

If you are in a relationship with another human being, you will be hurt by them, whether intentionally or unintentionally. How should you respond? Always use the "F" word. Forgive! That's really why Jesus came into the world to offer the "F" word to sinners like you and me! In his image, learn to forgive, sacrifice and always give all to your relationship.

HOMEWORK

1. When you read Ephesians, did that kind of love resonate with how you feel about the woman you are with? If not, why not?

2. How do you show sacrificial love in your relationship with your lady? Are there areas that you might need to improve in?

3. Name a sacrifice you are willing to make for your lady? Are there limits to this sacrifice that you have made either verbally or even internally to yourself?

Chapter 2

Selfless Love

That I.S. Affectionate

Once again, we turn to a cautionary tale in one of Bruno Mar's songs; *Grenade*. This details what happens to a relationship without selfless love:

> *Now my baby's dancing*
> *But she's <u>dancing</u> with <u>another</u> man*
> *My pride, my ego, my needs, and my <u>selfish</u> ways*
> *Caused a good <u>strong</u> woman like you to walk out my life*
> *Now I never, <u>never</u> get to <u>clean</u> up the mess I made, oh*
> *And it <u>haunts</u> me <u>every</u> time I <u>close</u> my eyes*
> *It all just <u>sounds</u> like ooh, ooh ooh ooh ooh*
> *Mm, too young, too dumb to realize*
> *That I <u>should</u> have <u>bought</u> you flowers*
> *And held your hand*
> *Should have gave you all my hours*
> *When I had the chance*
> *Take you to <u>every</u> party 'cause all you <u>wanted</u> to do was dance*
> *Now my baby's dancing*
> *But she's <u>dancing</u> with <u>another</u> man*
>
> *Although it hurts*

I'll be the <u>first</u> to say that I was wrong
Oh, I know I'm <u>probably</u> much too late
To try and <u>apologize</u> for my mistakes
But I just want you to know
I hope he buys you flowers
I hope he <u>holds</u> your hand
Give you all his hours
When he has the chance
Take you to <u>every</u> party
'Cause I <u>remember</u> how much you <u>loved</u> to dance
Do all the <u>things</u> I <u>should</u> have done
When I was your man[7]
Do all the <u>things</u> I <u>should</u> have done
When I was your man

Ephesians 5 "Love her like you love your own body.[8]"

Short Story for Consideration

Sam and Nora have been married for eight years. Sam is not a touchy-feely guy and makes a bit of a fuss when Nora occasionally tries to cuddle up next to him on the sofa at night. He complains that he gets hot and asks her not to do this. Unfortunately, Nora has met Raymond at work, a hugger, and tends to be someone she finds she gravitates toward to fill some of the voids she feels in the relationship with Sam. Attempting to stop any missteps on her part, she plans a nice meal and sits down to talk to Sam about this issue, as it continues to be a thorn on her side. He doesn't really respond much as he gobbles up the dinner, and when she brings up the cuddling aspect, he shuts her down, "we have a great life; why is that girly stuff needed for us as we are so good together?" He assumes the conversation is over, but Nora doubts if this relationship will go the distance, as she is not sure how much she can continue to sacrifice if Sam can't meet her halfway.

Hold Her

Men, hold her, tell her how much you adore her and what she means to you. This may seem like little stuff, but life gets in the way and our own goals, ambitions, and daily checklist of everything else we need to do allow us to let the little details slip by as unimportant or trivial. Yet, this reassurance to our lady that she is important enough for you to prioritize holding her every day despite all other distractions is critical to solidifying your relationship. Simply giving her a bit of affection at the end of the day, whether tired, weary from everything that went wrong and the obligations on your shoulder, will make all the difference. Women crave and need that connection, and if you can't provide this – they will look for it someplace else. Simple as that, but probably one of the things we all take for granted today the most.

We Don't Need to Fix It Sometimes

When your lady starts to give you a rundown of a situation, frustration at her job, something that went wrong with her day, or some other disorder, stop before fixing it. Sometimes, affection is simply listening, allowing her to vent, and giving her an outlet for the frustrations. We don't need to fix everything, and in fact, doing so quickly can seem dismissive and minimizing from her perspective. We are going for the selfless art of affection here, which means letting her be heard and providing her a platform for this without needing to be the hero. Sometimes, your lady just needs to have you listen; she might already know the course of action that should be executed but needs that nod from you that she was heard. That you gave her your undivided attention at that moment was most important to her. Winning brownie points on the scoreboard of affectionate displays could honestly be a simple nod of understanding and making her know she has you there when she needs you.

Weaker vessel[9]

Yes, God made men physically stronger than women. That does not mean to hold this dominance over our lady; rather, true selfless love says to use this strength to protect your woman. They might better you in emotional, intellectual contexts from time to time, so use this strength that was provided to you alone as a shield for your lady from abuse, in any form, from others or yourself. Submission to the selfless love for your lady says this is used positively to safeguard the relationship and should not be taken as a slight to use against your lady in any manner.

God has made the male stronger than the female, so when you see someone threaten your lady or influence her body in any way, it is your job to ensure that does not continue. Again, this body strength will not always translate to being smarter or wiser, as each relationship is a give and take. This blending of strengths and weaknesses help shore up a relationship to the strength of combined persons that cannot be torn apart.

Treat Her Delicately Like an Expensive Vase

Have you ever seen an expensive piece of crystal or a vase, and it is stamped, *handle with care*? Our wives come with similar better care needed instruction manuals throughout the Bible that we need to execute in our lives to be successful in loving our ladies. They deserve all the affection we can give them and none of the frustration, anger, malaise that the world imposes on us from so many areas of our lives. Remember, this is a helpmate, companion, and person. We should sacrifice everything to ensure their happiness and comfort. How much more important than an expensive vase are they? So, if you can place that vase up out of the reach of those who might bump, damage, or even try to steal it, shouldn't those same protection principles apply to our wives?

The affection, protection, and care we grant our wives' emotions, feelings, and entire being will pay dividends in caring for our needs. Additionally, the love born of these actions, remember, is on par with the agape love of the will. Love that has been poured out on us as sinners, that we, in turn, should, in full measure, visit upon our wives.

HOMEWORK

1. Do you treat your wife like a delicate vase? If not, what are the areas you feel might require some improvement for you personally?

2. Do you protect your wife with your strength, as discussed here, or are there moments when you use it against her? Is this an area of improvement for you based on the insights discussed?

3. In what ways do you show your wife affection? Is there maybe something more in this area you need to consider doing?

Chapter 3

Serving Love That Is Conversational

The Saturday Evening Post, years ago, posted this snippet about the Seven Stages of a Marital Cold[10]

> ***1st year cold:*** *The husband said, "Sugar dumpling! I'm really worried about my baby girl! You've got a bad sniffle, and there's no telling about these things with all the strep going around. I'm putting you in the hospital this afternoon for a general check-up and a good rest. I know the food is lousy there, so I'll be bringing you food from Tosini's. I've already got it all arranged with the floor superintendent."*
>
> ***2nd year cold:*** *"Listen, darling! I don't like the sound of that cough! I've called Dr. Miller to rush over here. Now you go to bed like a good little girl just for Poppa."*
>
> ***3rd year cold:*** *"Maybe you better lie down, Honey. Nothing like a little rest when you feel lousy. I'll bring you something. Do you have any canned soup?"*

4th year cold: "Now look dear, be sensible! After you've fed the kids, washed the dishes, and finished vacuuming, you'd better lie down."

5th year cold: "Why don't you take a couple of aspirin?"

6th year cold: "If you'd just gargle or something, instead of sitting around barking like a seal!"

7th year cold: "For Pete's sake, stop sneezing! Are you trying to give me pneumonia!?"

Ephesians 5:29 (NIV) *"After all, no one ever hated their own body, but they feed and care for their body, just as Christ does the Church."*

Short Story for Consideration

Bob is a monosyllabic kind of guy that is more miserly with his words than his hard-earned money. When he was first dating Sarah, he had, of course, made an effort to woo her with the help of some friends that fed him tips and tricks. As time went on, though, and they settled into their routine, he assumed she knew how much he loved her, as he provided for everything she could want. They had a nice house, lived in a good school district, and he worked long hours in his financial advising capacity to provide these things. Sarah, though, finds the silence between them problematic.

As time passes, talking only to the children and friends, she starts to notice herself making more decisions on household items without Bob. Soon, they don't even make an effort, as she puts the kids to bed and is resting by the time he comes home at night. Leading separate lives, until one day she realizes that she doesn't even know the man who comes home to her at night, and serious doubts start to formulate about where they will be down the road. Of course, she turns to those trusty friends for advice, and soon those voices take hold, and she visits a divorce attorney to explore her options, as Bob continues along, happy, in his reality of the situation.

The Importance of Giving Her Conversation

Women speak more than men, and they find their connections in conversation and connections. She needs 15 hours of meaningful conversation each week. This is not just passing niceties as you head on out to work or grunts of acknowledgment when asked about how things were during your day – 15 hours of meaningful conversation. Discuss your hopes, dreams, and in-depth day-to-day check-ins with each other to start. This isn't negotiable if you will foster that affection, love, and emotional connection women crave. Yes, men, this also, in turn, allows you to garner respect from them for taking this time to focus on their needs, and both of you win in the end.

Listen, your wife or girlfriend, more than anything, needs to feel your love. It is exceedingly difficult for a female to respond to a male when she does not feel loved. Her feeling of your love is as important to her as the air she breaths. Never withhold your love because she will suffocate. One of the most critical ways to show this love is conversing with her and connecting on a level no other being can. The rewards of love are immeasurable if you do this.

Intimate Conversations

Intimate conversation is the next step beyond the normal conversation. Intimate conversation is personal. It reveals feelings, concerns, cares and is often emotional. The intimate conversation often occurs while dating and then drops off after marriage. Most women not only crave intimate conversation, but they need it. Men tend not to need it as much, nor enjoy talking intimately after marriage.

The intimate conversation does not occur when one partner is distracted by the T.V., radio, or something else. Intimate conversation is dedicated time set aside for the exclusive purpose of connecting about the day, problems, achievements, dreams, fears, and goals. Dr. Harley, Jr. recommends 15 hours of such conversation every week.[11] While that may sound difficult, it is a sound way to develop a happy marriage.

If you are familiar with the concept of the Love Bank, the intimate conversation is a great way to make love bank deposits. Men need to understand this and develop intimate conversation skills.

Those with a need for intimate conversation will fall in love with someone who can have such a conversation with them.

They will stay in love with the person who continues to have an intimate conversation.

What Care Looks Like

Ephesians 5:28 (NIV) says, *"In this same way, husbands ought to love their wives as their own bodies. He who loves his wife loves himself."* In the same way, husbands ought to love their wives as they love their bodies. A man who loves his wife shows love for himself. Verse 29 of that same Bible verse states, *"After all, no one ever hated their own body, but they feed and care for their body, just as Christ does the Church."*

What Does That Mean?

You care for your body. Whose teeth do you brush in the morning? Whose hair do you comb? Whose body do you clothe? You take care of yourself. That's a given; that's a given. He's not saying, "Learn to take care of yourself" - some of you need to learn to do that a little better than you're doing it - but for the most part – for the most part, you feed yourself, you wash, you do what you're supposed to do for yourself. And what our Lord is saying here, through the Holy Spirit and the instruction from the apostle Paul, is give the same attention to yourself to your wife because you're one flesh. And do it - verse 29 says - because if you don't, it's a kind of self-suicide - you're hating yourself.

No one hates his own body but feeds and cares for it, just as Christ cares for the church. (Nourish & Cherish Her) The idea is to nourish and cherish your own wife, as stated in verse 29.

Nourish: this means to provide what will bring life and growth and well-being; and cherish: literally to make warm.

I guess you could, you sort of stretch and say to cuddle, to embrace, to provide security, and so there's this idea of caring, meeting needs, fulfilling desires. Nobody ever hates his own flesh, but everybody nourishes and cherishes it. Christ does that for the church, and you need to do that for your wife. The word nourish comes from ektrephō, which means to feed. It's a word used in the Bible primarily for nurturing children, providing nurture, providing a climate of growth and development.

You know, this is kind of the other side of the working wife situation - which is a serious problem, very serious problem - your wife is not supposed to provide for, and nourish, and cherish you. You're supposed to provide that for her, and 1 Timothy 5:8 says if you don't provide for your own family, you're worse than an unbeliever because even unbelievers do that. Something is seriously wrong when a man sees his wife as the source of provision for himself. Something is equally wrong when a man sees his wife as a cook, a washerwoman, babysitter, and a physical partner.

A man has to see his wife as a treasure to care for, to cherish, nourish, in the same way, the Lord does His church. Throughout Scripture, the man is the provider; the man is the protector, the man is the preserver, the man is the nourisher, the cherisher, as Christ is for His Church. The church really provides nothing; we cast all our care on Him; he cares for us.

Even the curse demonstrates that the man will be the provider because he is cursed in his labor, isn't he?

This is how a marriage becomes everything that people want a marriage to be, and so much of it lies in the fulfillment and responsibility of the husband and wives; they rest in all of this care and provision. So, it's a sacrificial love, it's a purifying love, it's a caring love, and finally, it's an unbreakable love.

HOMEWORK

1. How many hours a week of meaningful conversation did you have with your wife last week? Do you think her count would be the same if asked? If not, how do you close that gap?

2. Think through your daily care routine yourself and the detail and attention that goes into such. Now, think through how much love, attention, and detail your wife got from you yesterday. Is there an imbalance someplace that might need to be worked on?

3. What is an area of caring for your wife that you think you could improve in today? What steps can you implement to put that in motion?

Chapter 4

Scorching Love

She Needs Honesty, Openness, and Transparency

Billy Joel wrote a song aptly titled *Honesty* [12] that speaks directly to this next topic in these lyrics:

> *If you search for tenderness*
> *It isn't hard to find*
> *You can have the love you need to live*
> *But if you look for truthfulness*
> *You might just as well be blind*
> *It always seems to be so hard to give*
> *Honesty is such a lonely word*
> *Everyone is so untrue*
> *Honesty is hardly ever heard*
> *And mostly what I need from you*
> *I can always find someone*
> *To say they sympathize*
> *If I wear my heart out on my sleeve*
> *But I don't want some pretty face*
> *To tell me pretty lies*
> *All I want is someone to believe*
> *Honesty is such a lonely word*
> *Everyone is so untrue*
> *Honesty is hardly ever heard*

And mostly what I need from you
I can find a lover
I can find a friend
I can have security
Until the bitter end
Anyone can comfort me
With promises again
I know, I know
When I'm deep inside of me
Don't be too concerned
I won't ask for nothin' while I'm gone
But when I want sincerity
Tell me where else can I turn
Cause you're the one that I depend upon

Short Story for Consideration

Stacy and Tim had the absolute best time traveling together, having long conversations, and sharing so much of their lives. Over time, she felt that everything was amazing, and they were working toward the day when she was certain he would get down on his knee and pop the question. Then one innocuous moment happened that changed all of this, and as she was going to visit Tim one day, she overheard him on the phone angrily discussing a situation with someone. She didn't want to intrude, so she paced a bit outside the door, and it became quite evident from some of the conversations that he had not been honest with her in any way. Traveling was causing him both money, concerns, and stress, as he didn't like being in crowded places. He confessed to the unknown caller that he didn't want Stacy to think less of him, so he just tried to hide these 'little nuisances,' as he told the caller, from Stacy to keep the peace and the amazing times they had together. She had to wonder what other things he wasn't sharing, and in a moment of clarity, she turned and walked away from Tim's door, realizing that she didn't know him at all.

Be H.O.T. (Honesty, Openness, Transparency)

Honesty, openness, and transparency give us a sense of security. When a partner shares their innermost thoughts and feelings, becoming vulnerable, they give a precious gift to their partner. It is no surprise that women tend to need honesty and openness more than men.

If you feel especially loved when your partner shares their soul with you, becoming vulnerable, you need honesty and openness.

Tied to an intimate conversation, honesty and openness take the need to a whole new level covering many topics. Very simply, there can be no secrets between husband and wife. Anytime I come across a partner talking about their privacy and needing their own space, I know the marriage is in serious trouble. They are trying to hide something, past, present, or future. Such secrets drive a wedge between the partners. How can any person fully trust another person when there are secrets?

Dr. Willard Harley, Jr. suggests a policy of radical honesty. Radical[13] includes:

1. **Emotional honesty** – reveal your thoughts, feelings, likes, and dislikes, especially regarding your spouse's behavior.
2. **Historical honesty** – reveal everything about your past, especially as it pertains to your weaknesses and failures.
3. **Current honesty** – reveal information about your day, calendar, and activities, especially anything that pertains to your partner.
4. **Future honesty** – reveal full details about your plans and goals.

Your wife needs you to be completely transparent and totally honest with her. For her to feel secure in the relationship, she needs accurate and truthful information. Undermining her trust will make her feel off-balance and distant. As the late Marvin Gay taught us, she needs to know "What's Going On!" "Heeeey, What's Going On?"

Rihanna sang: How about a round of applause. A standing ovation. Listen, if you are dishonest to your partner, you are making withdrawals from her emotional love bank. Lack of truth, honesty, and openness gives her many false impressions and illusions, so that it makes it difficult for her to know what to believe. When you tell her the truth, you build up her emotional stability and empower her.

Such honesty is rare today. When we date, we tend to put our best face forward. That's fine for an initial meeting, but you cannot continue misleading your potential partner afterward. If you married this person and still have secrets or things you don't want them to know, now is the time to share that information. Simply by holding back, your partner knows there is something. That uncertainty leads to questions and doubt. Doubt and uncertainty have a way of building walls between people. The only solution is radical honesty.

HOMEWORK

1. Honesty – be truthful now; how are you doing in this regard in all areas of conversation with your wife?

2. Openness – are there topics you still aren't' comfortable discussing with your lady? Why? How do you see a way through this barrier?

3. Transparency – are you able to exercise transparency? Does this result in the outcomes you hoped for or caused other concerns?

Chapter 5

Sensitive Love

Understanding

Ralph Tresvant sang about a woman needing a sensitive man, and it again says with lyrics what many of you don't want to admit aloud:

> *Listen baby, don't even waste your tears on that insensitive man*
> *There's better things for you*
> *I mean, what you really need is someone who cares*
> *Someone that's gonna be there for you*
> *Someone like me, baby*
> *Someone with sensitivity (Hoo)*
> *You understand?*
> *Can you feel it? Hey...*
> *Ooh, na-na-na-na...*
> *Girl, I know it's been hard since he went away*
> *And left you so sad, you cry every day*
> *Let me kiss your tears, erase all your doubts*
> *'Cause for you I'm here, you won't be without LOVE!*
> *Don't need a man that'll give you money (no)*
> *Come on let me show you just what you need, honey*
> *(I got what you need)*
> *Don't need a man that'll treat you funny*

You need a man with sensitivity, a man like me
Someone who can love you
Someone who will need you
Someone who will treat you right, like me girl
Someone you can hold at night
Someone stable in your life (ah baby)
You need a man with sensitivity, a man like me

1 Peter 3: 7(NIV) "Husbands, in the same way, be considerate as you live with your wives and treat them with respect as the weaker partner and as heirs with you of the gracious gift of life so that nothing will hinder your prayers."

Short Story for Consideration

Megan and Tommy have been dating for a while now, and it seems like Tommy checks all her boxes. Unfortunately, she has some especially hard cramps during her cycle this month, and he wants to go four-wheeling. When she says she isn't feeling good, he turns to her and says, "this is ridiculous, we had this planned for a while, and this happens every month. Can't you just take something, and we can go have some fun." Unfortunately, this isn't the first time such comments come up at this particularly hard time, and normally, she does try to suck it up and go along. Today, though, she just feels sad, and like maybe she needs to truly start rethinking if this is someone she can see being with if each month or so this will be a fight. What happens? She wonders if she ever would have children and influence even more on what he wants to do. She finally tells him to go on and climbs into bed to soothe her aching muscles and a bit of her wounded mind from the interaction.

Treat Her with Consideration (understanding)

The word and your wife are both difficult and need skill in interpreting. Unfortunately, your wife will not come with an instruction manual; this is a learn-as-you-go kind of scenario, and the better you learn and adapt, the healthier the relationship will grow. Dwell with understanding to live with; to remain with; to stick with.

If you are ignoring her, another guy might be giving her attention. If you are giving her problems, another guy is willing to listen to her problems. If you hang up the phone on her, another guy will gladly take her call. If you are too busy for her, another guy is willing to make time for her. If you make her cry, another guy is willing to make her smile and laugh. If you are unsure if you still want her, another guy already has it figured out. He will take her! Luther says, "Love the one you're with," the WORD says: Love your wives, and that means unequivocally being sensitive to what they need. This may come in the form of communication, understanding, or physical protection. Open, honest and transparent communication helps you figure out those needs and rise to meet them every time.

Women Are Complex

There is no person alive that would tell you are learning all you must know about your wife's monthly cycle, P.M.S. (pretty mean sister), mood swings, and changes that will come with age, and children are going to be easy. Of course, nothing you have in life came easy; you have to work at it, understand it and grow in your discernment. Whether it be your career, your spiritual journey, or your relationships – it takes work. Put in the time to fully understand and appreciate all the quirks that make your lady unique. Then find out where you can show sensitivity, compassion and lend support to build that foundation you desire for the long term. Remember, not meeting her needs goes against God's plan and directive, so how are you expecting to have answered prayers for your needs if you oppose God's decree?

Become a Student of Your Wife

Recall being a student in school? That entailed listening to the teachers to absorb what they were telling you. The same principle applies here; being a student of your wife means becoming a good listener. Listening takes patience. That doesn't mean doing so when it is convenient, easy, or can be done with the game in the background. Listening to learn about your wife means engagement in the conversation, showing interest, and having her open up to you in an honest manner, to which you remain sensitive and filter the feedback before she has finished. Remember, this is not the time to try and fix but learn only.

Think of this as a McDonald's Drive through an order for the needs your wife has. When she places her order, you need to ensure you fully comprehend what she has expressed. Repeat the order back to her. Know that what she is telling you and what you are hearing and storing completely align for the future. If she says X.Y.Z., for instance, and you hear X.B.B. and later try to act on that, she won't believe that you heard her, were listening or interested, and frustration is the only outcome from that interaction you can depend upon.

We must go back to school. Remember that men are fact-based listeners, but women are feelings-based. Those don't always translate to the exact translation of the same conversation. Ever seen a document translated from another language to English and read through it with a furrowed brow? The words are there, but the comprehension is lacking, and it doesn't register with your brain the way a native speaker would understand it. That is what talking to your wife is like, learning a new language of feelings and emotions that you have to train your ears and brain to comprehend and apply sensitivity where she requires it from you.

HOMEWORK

2. If we were to rate your listening ability regarding your wife on a scale of 1 to 10, what would you rate yourself?

3. If you were to put yourself in your wife's shoes, what do you think she would tell us about your listening? Good, bad, or needs a lot of improvement?

4. When it comes to sensitivity, where is one area you believe your wife needs this most? How are you doing in that area? How do you think you might improve?

Chapter 6

Secure Love

Financial Security

The word Pursue /pər'soo/[14] means:

> verb (used with object), pur·sued, pur·su·ing.
> - ✓ to follow in order to overtake, capture, kill, etc.; chase.
> - ✓ to follow close upon; go with; attend:
> - ✓ Bad luck pursued him.
> - ✓ to strive to gain; seek to attain or accomplish (an end, object, purpose, etc.).
> - ✓ to proceed in accordance with (a method, plan, etc.).
>
> verb (used without object), pur·sued, pur·su·ing.
> - ✓ to chase after someone or something; to follow in pursuit:
> - ✓ They spotted the suspect but decided not to pursue.
> - ✓ to continue.

This is how it starts when a man goes after a woman but not always how it ends.

Short Story for Consideration

Ava and Greg have been dating for several years and talking about marriage for a while now. Greg, during dating, has been a perfect gentleman, picking up the tabs though Ava would ask to help from time to time. Both have nice jobs, though Greg does better financially. Together, though, it seems they are fully aligned. Tonight, however, Greg has brought a pre-marital agreement of sorts he has drawn upon his thoughts regarding finances, and the contents left Ava shocked. He would manage the finances, but everything would be split in a percentage-based system according to their salaries. Neither would quit or change their roles significantly without permission from the other. They would split child expenses considered necessary fifty-fifty when that time came, and extras would be paid by the party who wanted them for the children.

It went on and on, and at the end, he said it was similar to the arrangement that his mom and dad had, and they were married a long time. He thought this would spare any concerns down the road. For Ava, though, it came off controlling and putting burdens on her. She had thought not to be there should they decide to have children. She had come into the evening thinking marriage and left the dinner full of doubts and confusion. This emotional state was made worse by Greg's anger over not understanding why this was not reasonable. Reasonable was not exactly what she had expected of her marriage, and it stung as she asked for some space to consider how the future might look for them.

She Is a FEE-male.

She will cost you. What do you expect financially from your spouse? Do you have plans financially that depend on your spouse earning a certain amount or higher? Do you expect your spouse to work when you are not working? All of these expectations need to be shared with your partner. It is no surprise that women often have an emotional need for financial support, even when they work or earn more than the husband. I'm pretty old fashion. A woman should never have to pray for money. Ask her husband. Her husband asks God.

Today, women are far more independent than they ever have been. The actual need for a man is less than it ever has been. Many women earn more than their male spouses. Even if that is the case, what are the expectations? Women tend to like a man that can provide or at least participate financially.

Suppose a couple is planning to raise children, the expectations of the husband increase dramatically. If they dream of owning a house or fixing up where they live, financial demands can increase. If they like driving nice cars, the same applies. There are many areas where financial matters are very relevant. Discussions in these areas are best done early and often.

Security also means unbreakable

As seen in Ephesians 5:31 and Genesis 2:24, unbreakable love states, *"A man shall leave his father and mother and be joined to his wife, and the two shall become one flesh."*

One flesh, indivisible, the indivisible number: one. Two becoming one flesh: an indivisible, intimate, indissoluble union. Two becoming one: "what God has joined together, let not man put asunder." Individual identity is lost; there is no more individual identity. We are lost in each other - leave and cleave - oneness of mind, oneness of heart, oneness of purpose, oneness spiritually, oneness sexually, that ends in a child that is a product of that union.

HOMEWORK

1. When you first started dating your wife, how hard was it to discuss financial issues? Has that gotten better in time?

2. On the scale of things, you would like to work on in your relationship with your wife, where are the financial issues? Do you mainly agree, seldom agree, etc., and what do you think can be done to change the current status if you think it needs some adjustments?

3. Do you have children? If so, how did this strengthen or weaken your ability to discuss finances and balance needs in your family?

Chapter 7

Loving Her SEED (children)

Family Commitment

"Living Together, Growing Together" by The 5th Dimension describes this thing called family perfectly in the lyrics:

> *Start with a man, and you have one*
> *Add on a woman, and then you have two*
> *Add on a child, and what have you got?*
> *You've got more than three*
> *You've got what they call a family*
>
> *Living together*
> *Growing together*
> *Just being together*
> *That's how it starts*
> *Three loving hearts all*
> *Pulling together*
> *Working together*
> *Just building together*
> *That makes you strong*
>
> *If things go wrong*
> *We'll still get along somehow*
> *Living and growing together*

It just takes wood to build a house
Fill it with people, and you have a home
Fill it with love, and people take root
It's just like a tree
Where each branch becomes a family that's

Living together
Growing together
Just being together
That's how it starts
Three loving hearts all
Pulling together
Working together
Just building together
That makes you strong

If things go wrong
We'll still get along somehow
Living and growing together
Still get along somehow
Living and growing together

Living together
Growing together
Just being together
That's how it starts

Three loving hearts all
Pulling together
Working together
Just building together
That makes you strong

If things go wrong
We'll still get along somehow
Living and growing
Just like we're doing now, together

Short Story for Consideration

Rene is headed out the door as Sean is coming in. She has to get the kids from soccer, and then they have Wednesday fellowship at church. Normally, Sean returns in the evening and isn't able to participate, so she is pleasantly surprised to see him here early enough to go with him. When she extends the offer, he just bounces his head back and looks at her, "I did my job today; isn't this yours as a stay-at-home mother? I actually came home early for a little peace and quiet on my own." Then he continues into the house after greeting the children. That sentiment resonates with Rene and sticks in her mind. She finds her mood off for the remainder of the evening and gets even more frustrated when talking to Sean about it later.

Family commitment Is Not Child Care

Family commitment is the active participation in the raising of the children with their moral and educational needs. Many women need help from the father to properly raise their children. Some of the help includes:

- ✓ Meals together as a family
- ✓ Attending church services together
- ✓ Playing board games together
- ✓ Reading to the children at bedtime
- ✓ Teaching the children about finances
- ✓ Planning and participating in family day trips
- ✓ Playing sports with the children

Parenting takes a lot of time and training. Schedules need to be adjusted for family events. Parents may need to take classes or read how to raise the children. Some of the key areas include:

1. Learn how to reach an agreement with your spouse. The two of you must be on the same page when it comes to the children.
2. Learn how to explain the rules to the children. No one parent should be the preferred or good parent when it comes to the children.
3. Learn how to be consistent. Don't let the mood of either parent allow rules to be broken or swayed. This can pit one parent against the other. Children will learn how to leverage a parent.

4. Learn how to punish properly and fairly. Spanking can be appropriate when done properly. Corporal punishment can be excessive, especially as the child grows up.
5. Learn how to handle anger. Never punish a child when in a state of anger. Develop the skills of emotional intelligence to recognize when you start becoming angry and act accordingly.

Boys play house, but men build homes. Boys shack up, but men get married. Boys make babies, but men raise children. A boy won't raise his children; a man will raise his and someone else's. Boys invent excuses for failure, but men produce strategies for success. Boys look for somebody to take care of them, but men look for someone to take care of. Boys seek popularity, but men demand respect and know how to give it. Boys do what they want, but men do what they are supposed to, and more. Lord help me to become a MAN!

HOMEWORK

1. What activities do you participate in with the family? Do you think others might strengthen that bond?

2. Are you and your wife aligned on family commitment concerns? Where is the biggest disagreement? Where are the places you excel in?

3. Do you find strains in balancing time with your wife and the family? How have you solved these in the past? Do these need work currently?

Chapter 8

Signs of Love

(The Five Languages of Love)

For the final topic of conversation, the song "When a Man Loves a Women" does a spectacular job tying up all these topics, leading to the love languages in this way:

> *When a man loves a woman,*
> *Can't keep his mind on nothin' else,*
> *He'd change the world for the good thing he's found.*
> *If she is bad, he can't see it,*
> *She can do no wrong,*
> *Turn his back on his best friend if he put her down.*
> *When a man loves a woman,*
> *He'll spend his very last dime*
> *Tryin' to hold on to what he needs.*
> *He'd give up all his comforts*
> *And sleep out in the rain,*
> *If she said that's the way*
> *It ought to be.*
> *Well, this man loves you, woman.*
> *I gave you everything I have,*
> *Tryin' to hold on to your heartless love.*
> *Baby, please don't treat me bad.*
> *When a man loves a woman,*

Down deep in his soul,
She can bring him such misery.
If she is playin' him for a fool,
He's the last one to know.
Lovin' eyes can never see.
When a man loves a woman
he can do her no wrong,
he can never hug
some other girl.
Yes, when a man loves a woman
I know exactly how he feels.

Short Story for Consideration

Amber loves to give and receive physical affection in the form of hugs and from her partner. She has recently started dating Ben, and things are amazing when they talk; he loves serving others, and they have done many volunteer tasks. One day, she notices he tends to back up whenever she tries to hug him with the excuse of sweaty or not a fan of hugs. He is great in so many other ways, though, and so one night leaves a tiny hint in the house in the form of a book her mother had gifted her, called "The 5 Love Languages: The Secret to Love that Lasts". He calls her with a chuckle and says he doesn't subscribe to that fancy stuff, and he is just what he is, take him or leave him. As she hangs up, Amber is pretty certain she knows what choice she is going to make.

Love Languages

Gary Chapman, years ago, talked about five ways humans best receive love from others. These are important to understand, as you and your man might not have the same love language, and acknowledging this early allows you to accommodate his love language in how best to communicate your love for him. Additionally, understanding the language you speak in – how you give this is important because if your man's language is different, this could cause disconnections in his understanding of what you are speaking.

- **Words of Affirmation** - saying supportive things to your partner.
- **Acts of Service** - doing helpful things for your partner
- **Receiving Gifts** - giving your partner gifts that tell them you were thinking about them.
- **Quality Time** - spending meaningful time with your partner.
- **Physical Touch** - being close enough to be caressed by your partner.

Love Languages in Relationships

As you can guess, love languages fuel the emotional health of a person. Getting and receiving their love and affirmation in the form they most ascribe to is critical. For this reason, you must go back to the chapter about sensitivity, listening, and again becoming a good student of your wife. Learning her love language and being able to deliver her affirmation of your love in a manner that will most resonate with her is vital for the health of your relationship.

This doesn't have to be big, showy, over-the-top declarations but simply another piece of knowledge to use. Instead of buying a gift for your wife for her birthday, maybe you volunteer at a cause close to her heart together or donate if that would talk more to her Acts of Service love language. Those small moments, coupled with knowing **your wife's love languages**, will make some big impacts. Remember to be a student, repeat when she talks to you, and pick up what she **tells** you like these love languages. Knowing them for both of you could make all the difference in the world to a brighter, more stable relationship than you could ever have dreamed possible.

HOMEWORK

1. Do you know your love language? What about your lady – what love language would she fall ascribe to?

2. What is something you do to let your lady know you acknowledge her love language? What has her response been to this action?

3. If your love languages are not the same, how have you found to both acknowledge and validate the language of the other?

Conclusion

Pursue Her Always

When a M.A.N. (not an immature male) wants you, he will chase you. He will pursue you. He will always take you out. He will always love you. He will never make excuses. He will make time for you. He will protect you. He will sacrifice for you. Not only will he open doors for you, but he will also open his heart by being honest, open, and transparent with you. You will never have to question his sincerity. Pray for this type of man. Wait on this M.A.N. Stop frustrating your life with "little boys" and immature males. Be patient. Be encouraged.

References

_____

[1] https://en.wikipedia.org/wiki/Teachme

[2] https://genius.com/Musiq-soulchild-teach-me-lyrics

[3] https://genius.com/Bruno-mars-grenade-lyrics

[4] https://www.yesmagazine.org/health-happiness/2013/12/28/the-ancient-greeks-6-words-for-love-and-why-knowing-them-can-change-your-life/

[5] https://www.gty.org/library/sermons-library/80-383/husbands-love-your-wives

[6] https://www.learnreligions.com/agape-love-in-the-bible-700675#:~:text=%20Agape%20Love%20%201%20A%20simple%20way,sentiment%20that%20demonstrates%20itself%20through%20actions.%20More%20

[7] https://www.popdust.com/bruno-mars-when-i-was-your-man-lyrics-analysis-how-sorry-is-he-really-1889669292.html

[8] https://www.happymarriagecoaching.com/marriage-advice/affection-sex-10-emotional-needs/

[9] https://www.crosswalk.com/family/marriage/relationships/weaker-vessels.html#:~:text=Peter%20uses%20the%20term%20%E2%80%9Cweaker%20vessel%E2%80%9D%20to%20point,security.%20Peter%20is%20reminding%20husbands%20of%20this%20relationship.

[10] https://www.heartlight.org/articles/200512/20051230_cold.html

[11] https://www.emotionalaffair.org/wp-

content/uploads/2012/03/Dr-Harley_basic-concepts.pdf

[12] https://www.billyjoel.com/song/honesty-5/

[13] https://www.happymarriagecoaching.com/marriage-advice/affection-sex-10-emotional-needs/

[14] https://www.dictionary.com/browse/pursue

Do you need RELATIONSHIP HELP?

Shawn McBride offers virtual counseling to clients all over the world.

Are you struggling in your dating, engaged or marriage relationship with:

1. Infidelity, trust issues, recovering from betrayal/affair?
2. Difficulty communicating or resolving conflict?
3. Feeling emotionally disconnected from your partner?
4. Talking in circles with your partner?
5. Feeling stuck & having the same fights over and over again?
6. Feelings of anger, bitterness & resentment?
7. Feeling unheard & misunderstood by your partner?
8. Not feeling appreciated/lack affection in the relationship?

We specialize in working with couples in the most difficult situations. Let us walk with you on your relationship journey and help you:

1. Work through the tough relational issues that you are facing.
2. Teach you and your partner new relational skills.
3. Teach you proven relational tools.
4. Guide you to create the kind of relationship that THRIVES!

No matter where you find yourself in your relationship, we will always listen to your story and professionally assess your relationship at the Couples Counseling Center. With our professional help, you can replace frustration, anger, and worry with deeper understanding, affirmation, and fulfillment in your relationship.

Schedule your appointment with us today and get the professional assistance you need for your relationship!

www.CouplesCounselingCenter.org

Shawn McBride Teaching Resources

Mindset Reset – ISBN: 978-1092500227
>Mindset Reset is a practical book that will teach readers eight core principles of mindset renewal that will significantly enhance their lives.

Handling Life's Struggles – ISBN: 978-1986754071
>This 31-day devotional will inform, inspire and impact the lives of every reader who is currently facing any life adversity.

The Power of Words – ISBN: 978-1514330388
>Readers will discover the importance and necessity of speaking positive words of affirmation into young people's lives and will find the dangers and ramifications of speaking words of death.

Beware of Bad Company – ISBN: 978-1484850039
>Beware of Bad Company is an eye-opening and practical book for people of all ages. It offers vibrant, sensible teaching on the importance of evaluating relationships.

How to Become a Successful Student – ISBN: 978-1505437607
>American children spend at least 16-20 years of their lives receiving formal education. How To Become a Successful Student enlightens young people with 26 practical and easy-to-remember principles from A-Z that will help them excel in this journey.

Know Your Worth – ISBN 978-1495453939
>Know Your Worth is an empowering & inspirational 365-day devotional book written to help teenage girls grow in wisdom and understanding about issues relevant to their stage in life.

The 5 Needs of Every Teenager – ISBN 978-1548093532
>Far too many young people today feel disconnected, ignored, and completely alienated from parents and adults alike. After 25 years of working with adolescents, McBride authored this important book to enlighten parents and caring adults on what teenagers need relationally and emotionally to connect with them.

Shawn McBride's 52 Object Lessons – ISBN 978-1088489000
  This book teaches you to harness the power of object lessons for those who follow you, whether they be your children, the children of others, or adults longing to know and understand the Lord.

The 5 Steps to Achieve Your Big, Hairy, and Audacious Goals – ISBN 979-8656384407
  This book will inspire, challenge, and teach anyone who has the inner desire and internal ambition to go hard after their BIG GOALS, BIG DREAMS, and BIG DESIRES!

40 Days with Jesus! – ISBN: 979-8640215441
  40 Days with Jesus was written to help Christians form the habit of daily devotion learning from our Lord & Savior. Because the words of Jesus are life-changing and timeless, the 40 daily lessons only focus on the words that he spoke.

All materials on sale on Amazon in paperback and Kindle versions.

Or visit:

https://truthforyouth-417873.square.site/

Made in the USA
Columbia, SC
07 March 2025